"Take a Look... There's Money All Around You!"

Zangba Thomson

"Take a Look… There's Money All Around You!"

The #1 guidebook on how to become a moneymaking machine

ZANGBA THOMSON

Copyright © 2016 Zangba Thomson; Bong Mines Entertainment LLC; Zangba Thomson Production; and Papiesolo Publishing. All Rights Reserved.

Library of Congress Control Number: 2015958202

ISBN 10: 0692593586
ISBN: 978-0-692-59358-5

Illustrator: Subrata Dutta

Printed in the USA

Publisher: Bong Mines Entertainment LLC

Bong Mines Entertainment LLC
P.O. BOX 1745
North Baldwin, New York, 11510

Attn: Emmanuel Dwekla
Managing Director | Head of A&R

Email:
Contact@BongMinesEntertainment.com

For Joshua with love…

Table of Contents

CHAPTER 1

You Are a
Moneymaking Machine

It's true what they say, "You can lead a horse to water, but you can't make it drink." This ancient proverb applies to everyone under the sun; so throughout this book, you will be given several key ingredients that will help you unlock that moneymaking machine inside of you, but it's going to be up to you to put them to use. Before that happens, know that your success begins, continues, and ends with you; in other words, you are the master key to your success. You are the main ingredient in your life. Only you can get up and walk on that hard road to prosperity. No one can do it for you, but you. You are, and will always be, the captain of your ship, the boss of your thoughts, and the master key that opens the door to you becoming a prosperous moneymaking machine. You set the wheels in motion, but no one ever said that it would be easy to accomplish your goals or dreams. Rest assured, nothing substantial in life will ever be handed to you on a silver platter.

You have to go out there and work hard for what you want like everyone else, so stop waiting for someone to give you that big break. You came into this world with a vision, and over the years you've nurtured that vision inside of your mind. And now the time is ripe for you to live it. Do not delay another moment because time waits for no one. Opportunity sometimes knocks only once, and then it disappears, hopefully to reappear again; therefore, use your time wisely. Work hard, but work smart. Hone your talent, and after you have overcome every obstacle in your way, you will realize that your impossible dream wasn't so impossible after all. Then your confidence will begin to grow, and your name will glow in bright, star-studded lights. The world will finally see that you are a force to be reckoned with. But before that happens, there are things that I want to share with you—key ingredients that will help you to become a prosperous moneymaking machine.

It's not by coincidence that you are reading this book. I wrote it just for you and everyone else who have a vision of becoming prosperous. But the first thing I want you to realize is that the "money" that's written in the book's title, *Take a Look...There's Money All Around You!*, can actually mean anything that you want it to mean. It can mean money, love, friends, opportunities, or whatever your heart yearns for because everything in this world is connected. I chose money because of its universal importance, and arguably, what materialistic thing has our civilization made that's more appealing than money?

When you realize that you are "the" master key to becoming a prosperous moneymaking machine, you will begin to see moneymaking opportunities all around you. Your old workout machine or the accumulated pairs of sneakers or shoes that you have trapped in the closet will suddenly become items that you can sell on eBay; services that you've been doing for free, for many years, will now have a fee attached to them, and you will start believing that money does grow on trees, which is technically correct because 75 percent of our greenbacks come from a plant, which produces a soft and fluffy fiber that grows into a boll. The plant yields cotton, which is then used to make money, which we use to buy goods, pay our monthly bills, and so on. And you might not know this, but the US Department of Agriculture reported that cotton production is a $25 billion-per-year industry in the United States, third to China and India.

Therefore, a plant produces cotton, and then money is made out of 75 percent cotton, which means that 75 percent of our bubbly ideas or services can be converted into making real money. Not too far-fetched, is it? This "75 Percent Rule to Prosperity" equation is really simple: plant + cotton = $$$; therefore, you + your bubbly ideas, talents, or services = $$$, meaning that you are equivalent to a productive cotton plant.

Everything that you envision or experience, from your ideas to your natural abilities and talents, as well as the services you can provide, should be viewed the same way a farmer views his crop, and then you should ask yourself, "How much money can I make from this idea of mine, from this service that I am offering, or from this talent that I have?" The answer should be a set amount that you want to receive, in exchange for the service or product that you are offering. Imagine being all that you can be and yielding all of the fruits that your ideas or talent produce. You will lack nothing but gain everything in return because you will be using your abilities to become prosperous. But there are secrets that I want to share with you—key ingredients that you will have to mix together to form an end product that you can use to become prosperous.

Well, you might say, "Brother Zangba, I don't have athletic abilities like, let's say, a Kobe Bryant or Lebron James; a savvy business mind like Warren Buffet or Bill Gates; or an inventive brain like George Washington Carver, Lewis Howard Latimer, or a Mark Zuckerberg or Steve Jobs. Can I still become a prosperous moneymaking machine?" Yes, you can, because each and every one of those above-mentioned persons is special and unique, and you need to start believing that you are too, just as no two snowflakes are the same, meaning that you are more than capable in doing something uniquely different and great, but only if you allow yourself to become one with nature, one with the universe, like that moneymaking cotton plant. What do you have to lose that you haven't lost already? Therefore, throughout the day, say this out loud, *"I am a moneymaking machine! I see moneymaking opportunities all around me! I am a moneymaking machine! I see moneymaking opportunities all around me! I am a prosperous moneymaking machine! I see moneymaking opportunities all around me!"* Keep repeating this mantra because faith comes by hearing. And pretty soon, you will start believing that you are indeed a prosperous moneymaking machine, and that's when the magic happens. That's when you will start seeing moneymaking opportunities everywhere you go, even when you dream at night—you will envision yourself walking on Prosperity Street.

If you put a ten dollar bill under the rug instead of spending it, that is capital formation. It represents ten dollars' worth of something that might have been immediately consumed, but wasn't.

—*Garet Garrett*

CHAPTER 2

Knowing Is Half the Battle

I found out about the "knowing is half the battle" phrase from watching the animated TV miniseries *G.I. Joe: A Real American Hero* back in the mid-80s. Every explosive episode ended with a public-service announcement, which highlighted a random child or children, who encountered problematic situations. And then the G.I. Joes would come to their rescue by offering timely advices, or they would completely remove the harmful obstacles from the children's path.

Here are some of my favorite G.I. Joe public-service announcements:

It's okay to be a chicken if you're smart. There's nothing chicken about being smart. If you stop and think, there's almost always a better way.
—Lady Jaye

Maybe you stink at baseball because you need glasses. Having your eyes tested may clear things up. Don't avoid a problem. Meet it and beat it!
—Ripcord

You can learn to water ski if you keep trying. That's because you quit trying...You'll never win if you give in.
—Scarlett

Don't be in a hurry to build your tree house. Remember, anything worth doing is worth planning.
—Quick Kick

Back then, G.I. Joe was one of the shows that played a critical role in my upbringing because Ron Friedman, the creator and writer of all four G.I. Joe animated miniseries, was consciously aware, like most of the writers in the '80s. He knew that a child couldn't grow without knowledge; so amid all of the action and violence, he sprinkled in lots of precautionary messages and made sure that the last thing that his young viewers remembered was "knowing is half the battle."

"Knowing" is half the battle?

Anything substantial that you want to achieve in life, whether it's obtaining a college degree, opening up your own business, or simply baking a cake, is made possible after you have gathered together all of the necessary information, or ingredients, needed to complete your goal or task. Everything there is to know about the field that you are venturing into needs to be acknowledged, and once that knowledge has been obtained, you have already won half the battle. But let's deviate for a second, and go into what the word "knowledge" truly means. According to *Merriam-Webster* dictionary, "knowledge" means "information, understanding, or skills gained from experience or education" and so on, and it can also mean "having the awareness of something" or "the state of being aware of something." Either way, knowing (*knowledge*) can also be viewed as knowing yourself or being aware of you, what you can or can't do.

If you know the enemy and know yourself, you need not fear the result of a hundred battles. If you know yourself but not the enemy, for every victory gained you will also suffer a defeat. If you know neither the enemy nor yourself, you will succumb in every battle.
—*Sun Tzu,* The Art of War

Are you aware that whatever it is that you are searching for has always been here, waiting for you to acquire it? But did you know that you must give something special (*an idea, service, etc.*) in exchange for it? In Ayn Rand's 1957 novel, *Atlas Shrugged*, one of its central characters, Francisco d'Anconia, poses an interesting question. "Have you ever looked for the root of production?" he asks. "Take a look at an electric generator and dare tell yourself that it was created by the muscular effort of unthinking brutes. Try to grow a seed of wheat without the knowledge left to you by men who had to discover it for the first time. Try to obtain your food by means of nothing but physical motions, and you'll learn that man's mind is the root of all the goods produced, and of all the wealth that has ever existed on Earth."

The beginning of all things is knowledge. Before the plant (*you*) produces cotton (*your ideas, services, etc.*), way before the harvest (*earnings, gains, etc.*), even before a single seed (*your plan or strategy*) is planted in the ground (*your mind*), knowledge must be diligently sought after, like a predator searches for its prey. Knowing what to do and the correct way to go about doing it are extremely important. So how is knowledge obtained? By reading books or getting instructional advice from experienced professionals. Once that knowledge is obtained, you have to put together plans or strategies on how to use what you know (*including what you can or can't do*) to obtain what it is that you are aiming for. And then you have to fearlessly go out there and execute that plan or strategy until you have what you want in the palm of your hand, but don't be afraid. You will meet up with unexpected obstacles, things that will make you want to quit, but don't feed into that negative energy or emotion. There's always a way out of any predicament, and this is the secret: whenever you encounter an obstacle, change for the better, and your situation will also change for the better. Don't be stagnant, especially in a world that's constantly evolving, and expect to fall, but every time you fall, get back up. Remember, failure is not falling down, but failure is refusing to get up, and recovering from any major setback takes time, courage, and patience. But during these troubling times, you should take it as a sign to unwind, a time to reflect on why you fell, what went wrong, and what could you have done differently.

Successful people have fallen down more times than their fingers can count, but they have all gotten back up every single time. Therefore, in the future, you will probably fall down again, but it doesn't matter because now you know that you have to get back up. And you shouldn't view falling as something evil, because it isn't. In actuality, it's a good thing or a blessing in disguise because falling produces experience, and you will need experience to become a prosperous moneymaking machine.

That's why, during a job interview, experienced candidates will always be considered first because they have the experience, whereas an inexperienced candidate is just jumping into the pool for the very first time.

Veronica Roth, an American author wrote, "No matter how long you train someone to be brave, you'll never know if they are or not, until something real happens." When you experience life, you are displaying who you are in real time and what you are made of. But sadly, some people never learn from their mistakes, so they end up making the same mistakes over and over again, while others are wisely learning from their mistakes and becoming breadwinners. They fell down many times; some fall more painful than others. But you know what? They cherished their falls and learned from them, and now they are experiencing a fulfilling life, filled with moneymaking opportunities.

When I first heard Donnie McClurkin's song, "We Fall Down," I appreciated its simple message: *we fall down, but we get up, for a saint is just a sinner who fell down and got up.* The song has a never-give-up attitude and an inspiring message that encourages everyone, including you, to overcome the obstacles that will most likely cause you to fall. But at this make-or-break point, when all hope seems lost, when you are trapped between a rock and a hard place, know that you must find a way to get back up. Even though nothing is written in stone, this act of always getting up after a fall builds confidence, which is a key ingredient that you will need to become a prosperous moneymaking machine. Confidence will enable you to be your best, and you will begin to soar to great financial heights. Now that you've been primed about potential obstacles, you have already won half the battle. Now all you have to do is execute your plan with confidence and make your next move your best move.

CHAPTER 3

Turn Your Line of Credit into Your Financial Ally

When I was in high school, I took my credit for granted and maxed out my first credit cards within months of receiving them because I wasn't aware of how important credit is, plus no one taught me about the importance of having good credit, until I graduated from high school and applied for an auto loan and got denied. The letdown weighed a ton, but I only had myself to blame. Instead of building up my credit in high school, I had foolishly turned it into my financial enemy. And when I couldn't afford to pay the debt I had accumulated, I fell in the red, and then the collection agencies began harassing me endlessly. I dodged their calls the best way I knew, but the fact still remained: I was a financial liability, a credit fugitive on the run, with no ammunition in my financial gun.

I was at home plate, batting in the low 400s on my credit score, and I was a high credit-risk applicant, even if I had an excellent cosigner. I was in desperate need of credit redemption because I looked at my line of credit as imaginary money, and I didn't value it because I got it free. So I spent it recklessly, like there was no tomorrow, on noninvestment items, such as clothing and sneakers, but those things got old and worn. Nonetheless my credit-card debt was still young and growing, and after each month of refusing to communicate with bill collectors, my debt birthed new wings and soared to even greater heights.

Back then, employers weren't checking prospective employees' credit history, so I wasn't in jeopardy of not finding a minimum-wage job, but it took me several years to eliminate my debt. And I can honestly say that my debt disbursements felt like child-support payments for a credit-card baby I had previously birthed.

I was in financial hell for a while, and then I decided to reverse my self-afflicted misfortune or die a financial death. I had to find ways of turning my line of credit from being my financial enemy to my financial ally. I had to obtain "the proper knowledge" on how to obtain good credit. So I read books and consulted financial professionals, and finally after paying off my debt, I was left with no credit history because it had been years since I last had any credit activity. So I took what I learned from the books I read and the knowledge gained from listening to credit experts, and I pooled it all together and came out with a basic strategic plan to become a key player in the credit-card game, even though I had previously failed.

It took lots of patience, discipline, and sacrifice to get back in credit shape. But I knew if I was to stay afloat, I had to play by the rules. So the first thing I did was something I never did before, which was following a strategic game plan. The first card I applied for was a BP gas card, and I was approved for a $300 line of credit. Even though the amount was small, I knew if I could successfully manage a small account, larger ones would follow. But here's the catch—*no matter what your credit limit is, don't let your charges exceed more than 30 percent of your credit limit.* I followed this rule faithfully and paid my bill each month, without one single late payment, and when my balance was paid off, I purchased more gas and continued adding necessary data to my credit history. After several months, I moved on to phase two, which was getting another credit card, but this time, I didn't go looking for it. The opportunity found me at a Macy's cash register, where I was standing in line to purchase my mother a Michael Kors handbag.

I had the cash, and I was ready to buy, but then the cashier asked, "Would you like to apply for a Macy's credit card?" I thought about it for a second, and then I replied, "Why not?" But deep down I wasn't too sure if I was going to get approved because of my past credit history. As a matter of fact, I didn't think I was going to be approved at all. Then after a few minutes, the cashier said, "Wow, it went through, and you've been approved for $500 store credit!" She was extremely happy because my approval gave her the first credit account she had opened that day, so she was one account up on meeting her daily quota. I breathed a sigh of relief, and then I thought about all the months I had successfully paid my BP card and about how my strategy was finally paying off. Even though it was a minor victory, it meant a lot to me. And that day I ended up paying off 90 percent of my purchase in cash, and I put the remaining 10 percent on my new Macy's card, which I paid off using the same formula that I used to pay off my BP gas card.

I felt a sense of accomplishment, and shortly after that financial victory, I moved on to phase three, which was obtaining another credit card, to help boost my credit score. This time, just like before, I received another opportunity at a Best Buy cash register. I was buying my godson a brand-new PS-Vita handheld console. And just like my Macy's trip, I had the cash, but then the cashier asked, "Would you like to open a Best Buy credit account?" With confidence I said, "Let's do it!" He checked my credit, and within minutes, Best Buy approved me for a $2,500 line of credit. When the cashier told me how much I've received, I didn't believe him, so I asked, "Can you say that again?" He repeated, "$2,500!" That's when I knew that whatever I was doing, I had to keep on doing it because the results were turning out in my favor. And just like before, I paid off 90 percent of my purchase, and I put the remaining 10 percent on my new Best Buy store card, which I paid off using the same formula that I used to pay off my BP and Macy's credit cards.

I felt financially confident, as if I was standing on top of a heap of cash, and then my brother told me about CreditKarma.com, a website that offers free credit scores, reports, and monitoring, along with some other handy financial tools that helped me make sense of my credit. After signing up, I was shocked to see that I wasn't batting in the 400s any longer, and now I had a good credit score of 660, according to TransUnion. All it took was a year and a half to get there. Plus, the good thing about Credit Karma is it suggested credit cards with great approval odds, based on my credit score. I decided to try one of their suggestions, and I applied for a Discover It card. I figured I had two store cards and a gas card in my wallet, so it made sense to apply. I filled out the application, via a link from Credit Karma, and shortly afterward, I was prompted to call Discovery It to verify my information because I had gotten approved. I was so excited that I yelled out loud, and because I wasn't in the woods, I was told to keep the noise down. When I finally got on the phone with a Discovery It employee, after successfully navigating through their automotive system, he told me that I was approved for a $7,500 line of credit. I couldn't believe it, so I asked, "Can you repeat that again?" He replied, "$7,500, sir." I remembered smiling; I felt good because I had gone from $0 to $7,500 real quick, and I felt good about it. Then months after that, I received another card for $9,500. I can honestly say that all of this was made possible because I received the credit knowledge that I needed, then I formulated a bulletproof strategic plan, and then I executed that plan successfully. I believe you can too. It's that simple. Having an excellent line of credit will not only help you become a prosperous moneymaking machine, but it will also save you lots of cash if you use the credit to your advantage.

CHAPTER 4

Live Within Your Means

About a decade and a half ago, a friend of mine told me, "Don't obtain what you can't maintain!" And ever since then, his statement has resided inside of my head, among other wise words and sayings. But what exactly did my friend really mean? At the time, I soaked in his knowledge, never fully understanding what it meant, but now when I look back, I realize he was talking about living within your means, which could be defined as being "aware" of what you can or can't afford, what you can or can't protect, what you can or can't do, and so forth. And not living within your means simply denotes that your current expenses have surpassed your spending budget, or as my friend put it, "You just purchased a gold chain, but you don't have the muscle, or the respect, to keep a robber from taking it from you!" And if you're not careful, living outside of your means could lead you into accumulating unwanted debt or, in worst-case scenario, losing what you have worked so hard for.

I recently came across an interesting statistic. Pew Charitable Trusts conducted a poll of 7,000 US households, and in their studies, "More than half of Americans still break even, or live beyond their means each month." The exact percentage is 55 percent of Americans are most likely on the brink of debt, or they are already knee-deep in it. But this doesn't have to be this way, and if you are one of those Americans, I want to tell you that you can live within your means and save time and energy and, most important, money. For far too long, you've been putting cash inside of a wallet that has holes in it, and at the end of every month, you don't know where all of your money has disappeared. At this point, you've probably lost thousands of dollars already, but all hope isn't lost. You still have time to patch up the holes in your wallet and save some of your hard-earned money.

Let's say you are earning $3,200 a month, your rent or mortgage payment is $1,200 a month, and your other bills (*cable, electricity, water, etc.*) sum up to $1,000 a month. Your rent or mortgage payment plus your utility bills are $1,200 plus $1,000, which equals $2,200, so you have an extra $1,000 floating around every month. So what should you do with all this extra cash? I suggest saving 20 percent (*$200*) of that amount (*$1,000*) every month, and after a year of saving, you would have a total of $2,400 in your bank account (*plus interest*), more than $4,800 (*plus interest*) in two years' time and more than $7,200 (*plus interest*) in three. Do you see where I'm going with this? You can actually build your own 401K savings plan because the sky isn't the limit, it's only the beginning, and you can define your own financial boundaries by setting limits to your unnecessary spending habit.

Remember, you are a prosperous moneymaking machine, but in order to safeguard the money that you are making, you have to get the "knowledge" on how to effectively manage it, either from knowledge gained from reading money-management books or from consulting a money-managing expert. In addition to those two things, I suggest activating your willpower. Learn how to say, "No, I don't need this" or "No, I don't need that," and only spend money on simple things that you need. The simple life is the best life. This basic concept, when it solidifies or becomes a habit, will aid you in being the best moneymaking machine that you can be. But I know it's easier said than done, and that's why you have to exercise your higher self, to overcome your material wants and temptations. You have to know how to defeat your unnecessary spending thoughts, by throwing them in the sea of no return.

Every single day, new merchandises are being manufactured, and chances are you will be tempted to buy some of them. There's nothing wrong with that, if you can afford to do so, but if you can't, then you are *living beyond your means* and doing yourself and your bank account a total disservice.

I remember growing up in Jamaica, a neighborhood in Queens, New York, during a prolific time when hip-hop was an emerging genre to be reckoned with. The climate was extremely robust, like other urban communities on the East coast, where "dressing fly" (*wearing new clothes*) was the fashionable thing to do, and being a part of the in-crowd was equivalent nowadays to having lots of cohesive followers on Twitter, Facebook, Instagram, and the like. Having athletic ability helped, but I was a scrawny little teenager, and no matter who you were back then, you either had to have the gift of gab or a heap load of cash to get the girl. So from the very beginning, I had the odds stacked against me. I wasn't athletic, I didn't have a heap load of cash, and I was still trying to figure out how to ask a girl out.

But luckily for me, a girl thought I was cute enough and asked me out, and that's how I obtained my first girlfriend.

Around that time, my sister and I were being raised solely by our mother, and she didn't always have the money to keep us in the newest wears, but she always kept us looking clean in clothes that she could afford, all of which I am extremely grateful and appreciative for. But there were children who wanted more than their parents could afford, so they started selling drugs and living beyond their means. They started coming to school in designer clothes and shoes, and I'm not going to lie—there were times when I was tempted to follow in their footsteps, just so I could stay up to date in all the fly clothes and sneakers. So I tried selling drugs, but that lifestyle didn't fit who I was as a person. Maybe I was just too sincere and caring to be a drug dealer, or maybe it was my mother's upbringing or my grandmother's prayers.

After a week, I lost interest in selling drugs and began concentrating more on my writing, and looking back now, I can honestly say all the things that I've done, while in the streets, can be summarized as my education in the school of hard knocks, an experience that no school or university can teach—real-life hands-on training. I've learned that it doesn't matter if you're a street hustler or a corporate executive, you are setting yourself up for failure if you don't live within your means.

I remember wanting Magic Johnson's Converse sneakers badly, when they came out in 1988, but my mother couldn't afford to buy them for me. So this is what she did: she bought me a basic gray-and-white pair from Models. Even though it wasn't sponsored by Magic Johnson, it was still one of Converse's all-star classic releases of 1987, and I had no choice but to settle for them. I wore them to school with pride every single day because I was grateful to have on a pair of new sneakers, even though they weren't the pair I initially wanted.

I didn't know back then that my mother was teaching me how to live within my means, and then years later, she got me my first job in a busy supermarket on Queens Boulevard and then at a retail store, which was similar to the dollar stores that you see nowadays. I was a moneymaking, minimum-wage machine, making a whopping $4.25 an hour *(yeah, I know, tell me all about it)*. Those jobs were very crucial in my life because they gave me a sense of pride. I was making my own money, the straight and narrow way. And each year after that, my willpower grew bigger and bigger, and I thank my mother for that.

Therefore, the point I'm making is this—the first step to living within your means is utilizing your willpower, to just saying no to your unnecessary spending habit and then diagramming your income by jotting down where your expenditures are going. After carefully analyzing your cash flow, you will clearly see where your monetary problem lies or which areas you need to improve on or adjust.

In a sense, you will be creating a budget, which is an estimation of your income and expenditures for a set period of time, and budgeting will come in handy because it will help you set up your spending boundary. In Proverbs 8:29, "God gave the sea its boundary so the waters would not overstep his command," and you need to also think in this same divine way and set a boundary to your unnecessary spending habit, so it doesn't accumulate into bad debt. [Side Note: *Good debt is what your credit is built on. The longer your history of good debt is, the healthier it is for your credit score.*]

In summary, relief comes to a person who balances his or her finances. Don't you want to live a happier and healthier life as a prosperous moneymaking machine, with little to no financial worries and enjoying with your family a little bit more than before? If your answer is yes, then practice living within your means, and as you grow financially, your life will also expand. The transition will cost you nothing, but it will save you every penny.

CHAPTER 5

Invest in Yourself

My mother has a very sweet and gentle soul. And every now and then, she would tell me, "What God has for you, no one can take away." And just recently, I realized that her statement is true. And it's also a unique definition of the word destiny: the events that will necessarily happen to a particular person or thing in the future. My mother gave me hope every time she mentioned her encouraging statement. She didn't say it once or twice but over and over again, over time, until I understood what she was saying. And that's the power of autosuggestion. It made me believe that something good was going to happen to me in the future. Even though it didn't happen overnight, it happened eventually and I am grateful to my mother for that.

Miraculous things can happen when you invest in yourself, whether it's your time, energy, money, or any type of love that you show toward yourself. These self-investments will aid you in becoming the best moneymaking machine that you can be. But first, you must view your physical body as a moneymaking vehicle, and its engine is your mind.

The maintenance of your mind and body determines if you will succeed on the road to prosperity. Crucial things, such as eating right, exercising regularly (*yoga, running, etc.*), meditation, and getting the proper rest, are all necessary ingredients in maintaining the health of your mind, body, and soul. What you put in is what you're going to get out, and what good is a moneymaking machine that isn't working properly? So do yourself a huge favor, and do things the right way, so your mind and body doesn't travel down the wrong paths.

Generally speaking, investing in yourself is the best thing you can do. Anything that improves your own talents; nobody can tax it or take it away from you. They can run up huge deficits and the dollar can become worth far less. You can have all kinds of things happen. But if you've got talent yourself, and you've maximized your talent, you've got a tremendous asset that can return ten-fold."
—Warren Buffett

Here's a list of twelve great investments and lifelong assets that will help you to keep your mind, body, and soul happy.

1. Invest in an abundance of patience

I believe patience should be the first investment because patience will give you the capacity to accept or tolerate delays, trouble, or suffering without getting angry or upset. But here's one not-so-fun fact: patience can't be purchased. You can't walk into a grocery store and ask a cashier, "Let me get a bottle of patience." It doesn't work that way. Developing patience takes lots of practice, time, and energy. You will lose your cool so many times before you can achieve a level of patience, but always remember, nothing in life comes easy, and if it does, run far away from it.

I remember I developed patience because of gardening. The practice of growing and cultivating plants forced me to follow nature's time, and not what my watch was telling me, and then I started to analyze the connection between a gardener and an author. Both of them have, what I would call, a planter's state of mind. The gardener plants seeds, and the author inserts words on to a computer screen. In their early stages, the gardener nurtures his or her seeds for months, until the first signs of growth appear. And on the computer, the author nurtures his or her story for months/years, and then it gets printed. But way before the gardener's planted seeds blossomed into plants bearing fruits and way before the author's printed books turned into best-selling novels, patience was applied. It helped the gardener and the author to remain calm during periods of growth and reproduction, and it can do the same wonderful thing for you.

But what steps did the gardener and author take to obtain patience? I can't really speak for them, but like I mentioned earlier, I can tell you where I developed my patience from—right inside of my flower garden, and maintaining it was extremely tedious, especially when I had to get rid of weeds and other unwanted plants, which seemed to grow on more occasions than I would like. But before that time, I used to get really angry at the task of plucking unwanted weeds out of the ground, which I later realized was equivalent to me removing bad thoughts from my mind. And after a while, I started to enjoy it, and instead of rushing like I did before, I started taking my time and being the best gardener I could be at the moment, and that's when the magic happened because I was eager to learn.

A garden is a grand teacher. It teaches patience and careful watchfulness; it teaches industry and thrift; above all it teaches entire trust.
—Gertrude Jekyll

While gaining patience, gardening also taught me how to become a diligent researcher because I had to find out what types of seeds to plant, how and when to plant them, and most important, which soil to plant them in. I was at the "knowing is half the battle" stage, and quite frankly, I didn't know I was operating with patience. Subconsciously, I started observing things in their proper perspective, and eventually I became good at doing background researches, which takes lots of patience because it's tedious and time-consuming, but a dose of patience helped me overcome all of that. Waiting for things to grow and blossom became easier and easier over time, and the daily chores of structuring and rearranging sentences or finding the right words to write reminded me of plucking weeds out of my flower garden, which, by the way, I suggest to anyone who wants to obtain patience, plus get better at editing.

Because I was accustomed to planting seeds, I knew my words wouldn't turn into books overnight; it would take some time, months or maybe even years, before my writings blossomed in a complete story. And this is how I want you to think because you won't become a moneymaking machine overnight, unless you hit the lotto [*laugh out loud*], but in due time, with the right amount of nurturing, you will surely blossom. And if you don't have a flower garden, start one today, or maybe even buy a little houseplant. Nurture it, take care of it, and as it grows, you will also grow in patience.

All things come to him who waits, provided he knows what he is waiting for.
—**Woodrow Wilson**

Some people say "waiting" is perhaps one of the hardest things to do in life, but with a little bit of patience, you can have peace, while waiting for long periods of time. The world has a rich history of men and women who have failed in their endeavors because they simply lacked patience, which is the virtuous ability to wait calmly for what you want. It doesn't matter who you are, the universal law of patience applies to everyone. Seeds must be planted and nurtured for months before growth can appear. Ideas must be nurtured and developed for months, or even years, before they can be fulfilled, but in the meantime, there is a waiting period, and some people have to wait longer than others, only because the duration of the waiting period depends on the importance of the goal being pursued. It could take days, months, or even years. There are no shortcuts to waiting, and you will need lots and lots of patience to become a prosperous moneymaking machine.

There will be times when you will get frustrated and probably want to quit before accomplishing all of your goals, but I strongly suggest that you keep on keeping on. Don't quit because winners have the patience to win, and quitters never win because they are impatient.

Don't Quit!

2. Invest in reading lots of good books

I suggest you read lots and lots of good books in the field that you are venturing into, self-help, fiction/nonfiction, and the like. Books are great investments because they can open up a portal into the minds of some of today's most influential people. For example, you might not live next door to Oprah Winfrey or have access to talk to her in person, but you can surely pick her brain by reading one of her books. Whichever topic or area you need knowledge on, someone of importance, in every conceivable field imaginable, has written a book, a pamphlet, or an article or blog covering that topic or area. Someone already did the groundwork, so all you have to do is read it, formulate it into your constructive strategic plans, and execute those plans, but if the topic hasn't been covered yet, then you are at the forefront to write about it.

3. Invest in building up your self-confidence

Building up your self-confidence, or self-esteem, is without a doubt a necessary investment because if you don't believe in you, who will? And that's where self-confidence comes in; it's that motivational force that will push you toward becoming a prosperous moneymaking machine. By now you should know what a difference a boost of self-confidence can make. With it, a person can succeed abundantly, but without it, they can fail miserably before completing a single project. That's how important self-confidence is. It's defined as a realistic assurance in one's own power, ability, or better judgment, but to me, self-confidence is that unseen motivator—that attitude booster that enables a person, big or small, to overcome fears and obstacles, during their long journey to becoming a prosperous moneymaking machine.

But how is self-confidence obtained and, most important, where can it be acquired? I believe in Napoleon Hill's philosophy that autosuggestion can aid anyone in acquiring self-confidence. If you continuously repeat to yourself that you have self-confidence, you will gradually influence your subconscious mind to think this way too. It's that simple.

All impulses of thought have a tendency to cloth themselves in their physical equivalent. The subconscious mind will translate into reality a thought driven by fear—just as readily as it will translate into reality a thought driven by courage.
—Napoleon Hill (excerpt from **Think and Grow Rich***)*

We become what we think, and it's not unusual for a person with self-confidence to think decisively. In his or her mind, the person will never doubt their ability to succeed, but a person who doesn't have self-confidence, he or she will think indecisively because subconsciously the person doesn't believe in his or her ability to prosper. J. M. Barrie, creator of Peter Pan, was quoted as saying, "The moment you doubt whether you can fly, you will cease forever to be able to do it." So every waking moment, you have to think, speak, and believe that you have self-confidence. Throughout the day, say out loud, "*I have confidence in my ability to be the best moneymaking machine that I can be. I have confidence in my ability to become a prosperous moneymaking machine!*" Many distractions will come and many distractions will go, but through it all, you must remain focused because you have to constantly train your subconscious mind to believe that you are a prosperous moneymaking machine. In doing so, you will grow in confidence, and your self-esteem will be at an all-time high.

4. Invest in thinking positive

In today's social-media friendly society, activities such as surfing the web, reading, writing, watching television, playing sports, exercising, dining, and listening to music have become some of our favorite pastimes. But what we need to do more of is thinking positive, which I believe is one of the key ingredients in becoming a prosperous moneymaking machine. At every opportune moment during the day, you should think positive thoughts, and in doing so, your world will dynamically change for the better.

Positive thinking is a necessity, a life-altering tool or strategy used by great men and women to achieve their goals. When people fulfill a purpose in their life, they didn't do it by luck or chance. They envisioned themselves winning beforehand, and then they fueled their visions with positive thoughts.

What you think can make or break you. So when negative thoughts enter your mind, immediately replace them with positive ones. You can brighten your day just by looking on the brighter side of things. You are the source of your misery and the creator of your joy, and choosing to think positive is a healthy choice because happy thinking equals happy living. You are where you are in life because of how you think. Negative thoughts can lead you down a moneyless path, but positive thinking can turn you into a prosperous moneymaking machine.

A few years ago, I heard a story about a young man who was interested in talking to a girl in his class. Every day he would see her, and his insides would yearn for her love. With great admiration, he would watch her from afar, and then one day, he mustered up enough courage and made up his mind that he was going to talk to her. Well, the moment came, but before he could accomplish his goal, doubtful thoughts entered his mind. "She's not going to like me," he believed. "She's into athletes, basketball and football players." He beat himself up until there was no more room in his mind to store another negative thought. Eventually, he became discouraged because he had allowed doubt to steal away his joy and self-confidence. Later that week, the girl he admired started dating one of the guards on the high-school basketball team. The young man mourned for days after realizing that his window of opportunity had passed him by. What he imagined happened. He invented the idea of her liking athletes, and eventually his worst nightmare came true. He thought himself out of the equation and created his own unhappiness.

Why am I saying this? It doesn't pay to think negative! Not for a second, a minute, or even an hour. All through the day, you should be filling your mind with how good you want your life to be, and before you know it, you will be living the life that you envision. And if you can dream it, you can live it.

Think
Positive!

5. Invest in focusing your aim

Les Brown, one of the world's most renowned motivational speakers said, "Shoot for the moon, and even if you miss, you will land among the stars; but most people don't aim too high and miss, they aim too low and hit."

The act of aiming or directing anything at or toward a particular point or target takes lots of patience, focus, and calmness. Just picture a marksman at an outdoors shooting range, and if you study his movements, the casual way he adjusts his rifle's scope and positions his firearm, you will see that he is relaxed and focused when firing a discharged projectile into the bull's-eye of his intended target, but not everyone is that disciplined.

So ask yourself the following questions: What's your intended target? What are you aiming for in life—is it becoming a moneymaking machine or obtaining a bachelors degree or getting a beautiful girlfriend or wife or, let me guess, the first person from your family walking on the moon? Perhaps you want to be a lawyer or a doctor or a superhero or even the president of the United States of America. Anything is possible, and you can hit any target when you focus your aim correctly.

According to one scientific fact, the human brain consumes up to 20 percent of the energy used by the human body, more than any other organ, but here's the thing: our brain wasn't created to multitask. Its responsibility is to focus on one task at a time. Trying to focus on two or more things at one time is called task switching, which according to Wikipedia, "Is a theory that assumes that once a task is implemented in the mind, it stays in a given state of activation until it has to be changed, such as when a new task is presented."

For example, let's say you're memorizing lyrics to a song, and one of your band members walks up to you to ask you a question. At that moment, you are task switching when you discontinue your current task of memorizing lyrics to fulfill your new task of hearing a question being asked. This proves that the mind can only focus on one task at a time, and according to a study conducted in 2001 by Joshua Rubinstein, Jeffrey Evans, and David Meyer, "Your productivity can be reduced by as much as 40 percent by the mental blocks being created when you switch tasks."

So why multitask, if doing so decreases your productivity? Why not invest in focusing your aim on one task at a time? Doing so will allow you to finish your job in half the time, but most important, it will increase your productivity as a moneymaking machine. But without focus, your mind will wander, and what you are aiming for will become blurry, making it hard for you to see—whatever it is that you are trying to obtain.

But staying focused takes patience, preparation, and lots of discipline, and it won't happen overnight. Here is a secret in staying focused and keeping your eye on the prize. Proverbs 4:25 states, "Let your eyes look directly forward, and your gaze be straight before you," which means you must discipline your eyes to always look straight ahead, at whatever it is that you wish to obtain or accomplish, and keep looking until you have obtained or accomplished that thing that your heart desires.

Stay Focused!

6. Invest in eliminating worrying

Everyone wants to feel at ease or be at peace, living a moneymaking life and not having to worry about problems. Some people want the luxury of knowing that when they are at work, their jobs are secured, their health is up to date, and their families are safe. Anything less than those comforting thoughts will cause a person to feel diseased, which is a worrying condition that produces mental discomfort.

Nowadays, worrying is at an all-time high. Uncomfortable situations are on the prowl, waiting for a victim at every opportune corner. Countries, states, and people are filing for bankruptcy, and in the minds of some of today's best financial analysts, the US economy is slowly falling apart, one-dollar bill at a time.

On television, we are constantly being reminded how terrible it is outside of our homes, so many of us are cautious when stepping foot outside because we are worried that something bad might happen. But life doesn't have to be this way. A peace of mind is what you will need to eliminate worrying. The more at peace you are with yourself, the more you will feel at ease, but your conscience needs to be cleared in order to experience a worry-free life. People and situations need to be forgiven, and you need to move on from your past hurts and disappointments because your future awaits you. So eliminate worrying, and be the best moneymaking machine that you can be. And always focus on solving your problems, instead of complaining about them. Find a way out of your worrisome predicaments, instead of being content with them. Wherever there is a will, there is a way out of all the worrying that you are doing. The light at the end of the tunnel may seem dim, but with a little bit of faith and determination, you will be free from whatever it is that you are worrying about. Always remember, in everything that you do, do not focus on your problems because focusing on them will cause stress, and over a long period of time, unhealthy thinking (*worrying*) will cause you to breakdown psychically, mentally, and spiritually.

> # Don't Worry!

7. Invest in being sincere

Telling the truth to others and yourself has its rewards. But where exactly does being sincere get you? Before I answer that, let's first define what being sincere is. According to *Merriam-Webster* dictionary, "sincere" is "having or showing true feelings that are expressed in an honest way"; "being genuine or real, and not false, fake, or pretentious"; and being honest, frank, and straightforward in your speech and thinking. To act otherwise is considered being insincere, dishonest, hypocritical, or deceptive. If we truly have love within our hearts for one another, then why is being sincere in today's society such a challenging task?

The answer lies in the little "white lies" and bigger lies that we tell every day, either to cover up mistakes, avoid embarrassments, gain financial wealth or material things, conquer a new love interest, or simply just being considerate, and not wanting to hurt someone's feelings. Whatever the case may be, the reasons for being insincere are endless. But how far can "not" expressing your genuine feelings take you? And are we obligated to tell the whole truth and nothing but the truth only in court?

No one wants to be disliked, so people have learned to polish their responses with a heavy sugar coating of insincerity, maybe to make someone else feel better, which is understandable, but oftentimes people are insincere because they want to look impressive, feel good, and be admirable to others. In either case, for better or worse, being insincere doesn't come from the heart, and it can put a chink in your moneymaking machine's armor.

8. Invest in being proactive

Procrastination is the act of deferring an action to a later time, and if you don't eliminate it now, it will prevent you from becoming that moneymaking machine that you were meant to be.

Charles Dickens, an English writer and social critic, was quoted as saying, "My advice is to never do tomorrow what you can do today. Procrastination is the thief of time." Dickens, after eliminating procrastination from his life, went on to write fifteen novels, five novellas, and hundreds of short stories and nonfiction articles. He couldn't afford to procrastinate, and according to Wikipedia, "His early impoverishment drove him to succeed (*I would say it drove him to become a prosperous moneymaking machine*)."

Imagine if Dickens had procrastinated? Memorable books such as *Oliver Twist, A Christmas Carol,* and *A Tale of Two Cities* would have been deferred. That's what procrastination does; it robs its victims of fame and fortune.

Nike, Inc., the world's leading innovator in athletic footwear, apparel, equipment, and accessories, knows a thing or two about avoiding procrastination, and one of their core components is "Just Do It," their highly recognized trademarked slogan, which is clear, simple, and to the point and can be viewed as probably one of the greatest three-word commands ever put together to overcome procrastination.

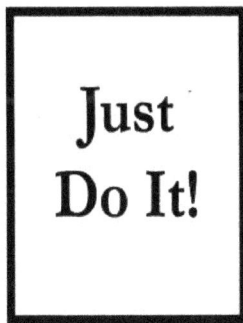

Just Do It!

9. Invest in change

Nothing stays the same. The world is constantly evolving, so you have to be able to adapt to change, way before it is necessary to do so. You must create a new you every day, being the change that you wish to see in the world. If you want peace, then you have to be at peace within. If an argument happens inside of your home, know that strife is simultaneously being poured out into your neighborhood, and eventually the world. Everything is relative—maybe not by blood, but everything begins within. Everything begins with a vision. It begins with you, and being a prosperous moneymaking machine will not only change your life for the better, but it will also change the lives of your family, friends, and others around you.

10. Invest in gratitude

Whatever you have now, be grateful that you have it, and in return, you will feel happiness within. A little gratitude can take you a long way. It can fuel your happiness. Therefore, take nothing for granted, and be grateful for everything, good or bad.

Be Grateful!

11. Invest in getting along with people

In grade school, I remember coming home one day and telling my mother I wasn't getting along with a couple of my classmates, and she replied, "To be successful, you have to get along with other people." That advice stuck in my head, and ever since then, I've been going out of my way to get along with people—even the ones who are next to impossible to get along with. But why should you go out of your way to do that? I'll explain. Teamwork is the cooperative effort by the members of a group to achieve a common goal. No one accomplishes anything great without the help of others, and chances are, without a good team, you will more than likely fail at becoming a prosperous moneymaking machine.

NFL's Hall of Fame coach Vince Lombardi said it best, "Individual commitment to a group effort is what makes a team work, a company work, a society work, a civilization work (*and a moneymaking machine work*)." So quit trying to do everything by yourself, and surround yourself with good people who can assist you in becoming prosperous. Remember, strength comes in numbers, and united we stand, divided we fall. And the only person you need to be competing against is yourself.

> **Teamwork**
> **Makes**
> **the**
> **Dream**
> **Work!**

12. Invest in being beautiful

In everything that you do, let it be done beautifully—when you think of someone, think of him or her in a beautiful way, when you talk to someone, talk to him or her using beautiful speech, when you create something, design it beautifully. Do things in a beautiful way so that you may receive beautiful results. Know that beauty is one of the greatest virtues; therefore, be beautiful in all that you say and do, and you will become a beautiful moneymaking machine.

**Be
Beautiful!**

CHAPTER 6

Talk the Talk, and Then Walk the Walk

I was standing next to a stranger one day, and I remembered him being clothed in neat attire. He was a very polite and articulate man. "Don't stop moving/Give it all you got/and keep risin' to the top," he joyfully sang the lyrics to Keni Burke's hit song— "Risin' to the Top," and immediately I felt a burning sensation, bubbling up inside of me. And then shortly after the man's departure, I realized he was singing one of the key ingredients to becoming a moneymaking machine, and that ingredient is activity, the condition in which things are happening or being done. Later that night, cuddled under a warm comforter, I read a document that stated, "Dreams are only fulfilled when dreamers actively pursue them persistently." Again, the word "actively" stuck out like a sore thumb, and that reconfirmed that activity is indeed one of the master keys in becoming a prosperous moneymaking machine.

And anyone, who has ever accomplished something of great value, will tell you that you have to remain active, in your doing and in your thinking, and you have to constantly be moving forward toward fulfilling your vision—no matter where your starting point in life is. You can come from the ghetto or a middle-class neighborhood, or you can be living on 3.7 acres in Beverly Hills. Whoever you are or wherever you are from, whether you're black or white, rich or poor, we all can talk the talk, but then after that we have to walk the walk. That's as straightforward as things can get.

I can recall years before one of my best friends passed away, he told me, "You ain't doing nothin' if you ain't sweatin'!" And he was right. I could talk about what I wanted to do all day long, but if I wasn't backing it up with action, then nothing was ever going to happen. Imagine me being idle, sitting in front of the TV all day, but still telling the world that I'm gonna do this and I'm gonna do that.

Yes, I'm talking the talk, but if I'm not walking the walk, then I'm only talking in vain, or as my friend would put it, "I'm talking out the side of my mouth." And that same concept applies to you, if you're not walking the walk, meaning that you're not going to get anywhere and nothing magical will ever happen without you moving to make it happen. As you move forward in faith, closed doors will open, and you will find yourself on the prosperous side of things, enjoying life to the fullest because you never stopped moving.

I remember one time when I had to walk the walk after talking the talk. It was in September of '08, a month after publishing my debut novel *Three Black Boys*. I ordered over three hundred copies. When they arrived, I stockpiled them in my bedroom. After doing an in-depth research on the book industry, I realized that I had to go out there and sell my books because no one was going to sell them for me. So my friend and I took a road trip to Harlem, New York, with 200 copies of my novel boxed in the trunk of my car. When we arrived, we didn't know where to start. So we asked many questions and a few people pointed us in the right direction. After hours of networking with vendors and storeowners, we received our first break. The owner of Hue-Man Bookstore liked my sales pitch so much that she paid me in cash for several copies of my book. I remember feeling grateful because her generosity gave me the confidence to continue walking the walk. And then a short while later, Black Star Music & Video store and a popular book distributor took many copies on consignment.

One week later, Black Star Music & Video store and the distributor were completely sold out of *Three Black Boys*. So the distributor asked me to do an outdoor book signing at one of his bookstands, located across the street from the legendary Apollo Theater. The sidewalks were jam-packed with people and the streets were filled with cars. We sold many books that day. And not too long afterwards, Hue-Man Bookstore set up an official "in-store" book signing for me, along with three other authors, and we were introduced as the new voices in Literary Fiction. Within a month's time, approximately 1,500 copies of *Three Black Boys* were sold in the streets of Harlem for $10 a copy. And then one month later, Molloy College hosted my first "Meet & Greet the Author" in Rockville Centre, New York. My mission was accomplished, and I felt great because I had walked the walk after talking the talk.

Recently, I gave a brief speech at my grandmother's funeral, and I spoke about how great of a prayer warrior she was. She prayed a lot, for each and every one of us living on planet earth, every day and all day. Her Bible was her favorite book to read, and she could quote any scripture at the drop of a dime. Because of her, I learned a very valuable secret about what to do before walking the walk. She told me, "It's very difficult to take a leap of faith when there aren't any grounds to walk on, but if you take that initial first step, then magically the ground will be provided." And ever since then, I've had the courage to walk the walk, and you can too, because the time is ripe for you to blossom into a prosperous moneymaking machine. You are the head and not the tail, and whenever in doubt, motivate your mind by saying these statements with conviction, *"I am a prosperous moneymaking machine! I see moneymaking opportunities all around me!"* Say them in the morning, afternoon, evening, and even late at night before you fall asleep. Say them until and even after you envision becoming a prosperous moneymaking machine.

Too often I hear people say, "I'm gonna do this, and I'm gonna do that. Blah, blah, blah!" But then nothing ever happens because they never followed through on what they said they were going to do. They failed to realize that talking the talk is synonymous with walking the walk, and words and actions go together like peanut butter and jelly or fish and ocean. First, we say what we want to do, and then we go out there and do what we say we are going to do. It's that simple. The talking part is the easiest, which anyone can do it, but the walking part takes hard work and dedication, day in and day out. Nothing ever happens until you make it happen. So take a look around. What do you see? Whatever it is, if it wasn't you, then someone or a team of people had to walk the walk to put it there. They made it happen, and you can too by making your next move your best move.

Oprah Winfrey once said, "Doing the best at this moment puts you in the best place for the next moment." By walking the walk and making her next move her best move, Oprah Winfrey went from being poor to a billions-making machine, and you can also reach that great financial height. Nothing is impossible, and while talking the talk, during any conversation, it's wise to always talk less and listen more to the person that you are conversing with. Keep your dialogue short and sweet, generally to a point where you are not blabbering, because Proverbs 10:19 states, "When there are many words, transgression is unavoidable, but he who restrains his lips is wise." When you restrain your lips from doing too much talking, you will be considered intelligent, but in the multitude of your words, your actual cleverness will be on display. Talking too much does more harm than it does good. Therefore, avoid excessive talking and listen more.

Another key gem to keep an eye out for is momentum, which is the powerful force or speed of movement. When you use momentum to your advantage, you are setting yourself up to be the most productive moneymaking machine ever. But without the help of momentum, it will be extremely difficult to achieve whatever it is that you are trying to achieve. For example, a high jumper approaches his starting point, then he takes off running with great speed, and then he gains enough momentum before jumping high into the air, eventually clearing the bar. Then imagine if he didn't move at all, but stood still below the bar, and tried to clear it that way. Would he fail or succeed? I believe more than likely he fails because no momentum is gained, and one thing is for sure: momentum would give him his best chance at clearing the bar, and it can do the same for you when you are walking the walk in becoming a moneymaking machine.

CHAPTER 7

Always Make the Right Decision

It may sound cliché, but it's true. Becoming a moneymaking machine is only possible if you are making the right decisions. In life, tough choices have to be made in order for you to move ahead. You, as a decision maker—*whether you like it or not*—have the hardest job on this planet because your decisions determine whether you become prosperous or not, and as you navigate through life's enchanted maze, opportunities will present themselves to you. And to the best of your abilities, you have to make the right decisions in regards to which direction to travel. But everyone's destination is unique, and some of us will make the right decisions, some will make the wrong decisions, and others will remain stationary because they are indecisive. But when making the right decision, the general rule is not to decide thoughtlessly. You need to think about your choices, and then reason them out thoroughly. Should you make a short-term decision or one that benefits you in the long run? Will your decision produce a positive result for all parties involved? Is this decision of yours something that you can live with? Please be sure, because you don't want to be haunted in the future by the consequences of a foolish decision that you make today.

If by chance, let's say, you make the wrong decisions and get lost on your quest in becoming a moneymaking machine, how do you get back on the right track? Is there a cheat code or something that can help you to get back into the swing of things? Yes, there is, and I will identify that intelligent agent in a moment, but first, let's discuss its man-made equivalent.

Have you ever driven toward a desired location using your GPS navigation device and, somewhere along the way, mistakenly made a wrong turn? Raise your hand if you've ever been guilty of that. I know I have. But what happens next is what I want to discuss. Your GPS automatically starts recalculating a detour route to get you back on the right track, and one GPS-assisted turn after another eventually gets you back on the right track.

This goes to show that you will only become a moneymaking machine when a consecutive amount of right decisions are made. Not one, not two, not three, but continuously. There will be times when you will make the wrong decision, which might lead to another wrong decision and then another wrong decision. And then all of a sudden, you might find yourself lost and trapped between a rock and a hard place, but don't panic. The easiest way out of your predicament is to make a right decision, then another right decision, and then another right decision, and sooner or later, you'll be right back on the path to success.

But getting lost should be viewed as a blessing in disguise because it forces you to make the right decisions, and listening to the voice of your GPS is the right thing to do because it helps you get out of your predicament. But there is something else—something more powerful than any GPS or artificial intelligence system, something that's been successfully guiding people ever since the beginning of time. That special something is your conscience. It can intelligently aid you in making the right decisions, and most important, it can tell you when you are right or wrong. And worrying is eliminated when your conscience becomes your default intelligent agent. But listening to your conscience isn't as easy as it sounds. It takes time, faith, and lots of obedience, because the right decision is always the hardest decision to make.

You might ask, "Brother Zangba, how do I know if I'm making the right decision?" You will know because deep down within your soul you will hear your conscience telling you that you have made the right decision.

A warm feeling of relief will resonate within you, and you will feel good and not be plagued with a guilty conscience. Your conscience will be cleared, and you will be able to laugh during the day and then sleep well at night. And most of the time, the key to living a good and prosperous life isn't too complicated after all. It's really simple, and all you have to do is listen to your conscience for the right directions on where to go. The more you listen, the sooner you will become a prosperous moneymaking machine.

ACKNOWLEDGMENTS

I would like to thank The Most High, The Highest—The Universal Prime Creator for giving me the right amount of wisdom, knowledge, and understanding to finish writing this guidebook; "hotep" (peace) to my Heavenly Father and Divine Mother, my family, my friends, and loved ones. I love you all! And always remember that (P) Positive (E) Energy (A) Always (C) Creates (E) Elevation (PEACE).

About the Author

Zangba Thomson is an urban, best-selling novelist. His creative works deal mainly in the realms of spirituality, metaphysics, and visionary, with a little bit of love and drama sprinkled in between. His image and creative works have been seen on or talked about in major media outlets, such as FOX 5, NBC, Today, Fox & Friends, Kathy Lee & Hoda, Arise 360, Shade 45: Sway in the Morning, ABC, Daily Mail (UK), Vibe Magazine, Centric TV, HOT 97, Essence Magazine, and The Tom Joyner Morning Show.

SELF-HELP/PROSPERITY

THIS MAY BE THE MOST IMPORTANT BOOK YOU WILL EVER OWN.

The #1 guidebook on how to become a moneymaking machine!

"Take a Look... There's Money All Around You!" is a prosperity, life-changing guidebook, which highlights the secret ingredients needed to become a prosperous moneymaking machine. Maybe you want to make 30k a year, a month, or even weekly. Or maybe you want the treasures of the universe. It doesn't matter. This practical, easy-to-read manual will show you how to become prosperous in seven straight-to-the-point chapters.

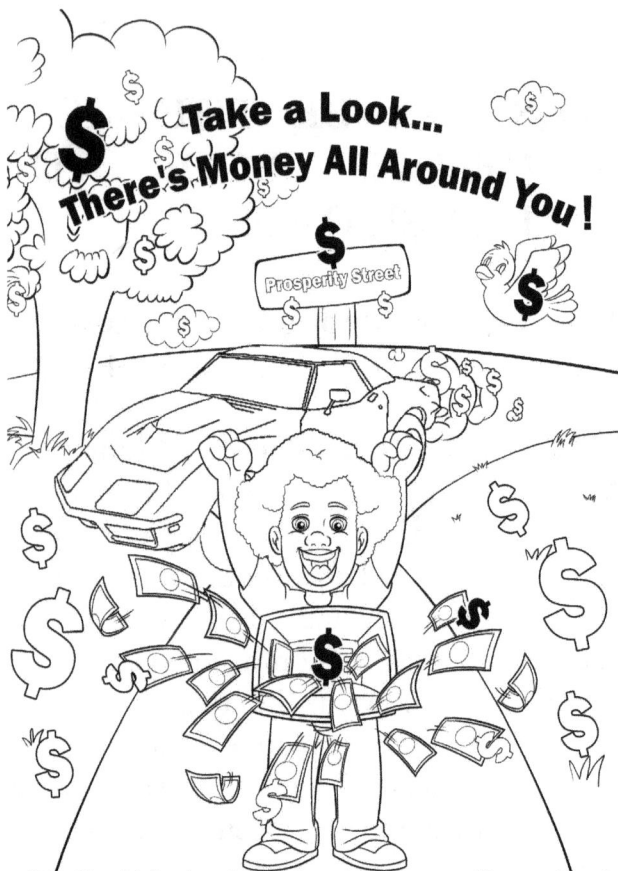

Take a Look...
There's Money All Around You!

Prosperity Street

"The #1 guidebook on how to become a moneymaking machine."

.